THE JOURNEY TO FREEDOM ON THE
UNDERGROUND RAILROAD

TEXT AND ILLUSTRATIONS BY
LOUISE CHESSI McKINNEY

To order additional copies of this book, contact:
Xlibris
844-714-8691
www.Xlibris.com
Orders@Xlibris.com

ISBN: Softcover   978-1-4257-2304-0
         EBook   978-1-6641-2688-6

Print information available on the last page.

Rev. date: 08/18/2020

This book is dedicated to my parents
Thomas and Alice McKinney.
Thanks for all of your help and support.
Also I dedicate this book to the memory of all of the people involved
in the journey of the Underground Railroad.

The Underground Railroad

The Underground Railroad began in the middle part of the 1800's and was an intricate network of routes, trails, safe-houses, and hideouts along which volunteer "conductors" helped slaves to escape the plantation, and become free. It often involved dangerous travel over land, mountains, lakes, and rivers. The Underground Railroad used a complex system of communication between the slaves, Masons, Abolitionists, ship captains, ministers, writers, blacksmiths, and free African-Americans. This form of communication is now known as <u>The Underground Railroad Quilt Pattern Code.</u>

The slaves worked from sunrise to sunset picking cotton on the plantation. They were very tired, and often wanted to run away from a harsh life where they were forced to work against their will.

When they could not take the hard life on the plantation anymore they often did run away. They would leave at night to avoid being seen and captured. Many times they would leave with only what they could carry or bring in a hurry.

Sometimes the runaways had to cross rivers and streams by wading through them. The water helped them to escape because it would often cover their scents and the plantation overseer's dogs could not find them.

The Appalachian Mountains offered them shelter and many safe places to hide. They were able to follow many trails to find food and water, and sometimes they were able to find a place to sleep such as an old barn.

The North Star was often the brightest star in the sky and it helped the people to find their way to the north. It also guided their paths at night and kept them moving in the right direction.

They would usually travel in the spring when the weather was warmer. Also the trees and bushes gave them places to hide when in danger or being chased.

Secret messages were sometimes sewn into quilts which told the runaways where to go or what direction to move in. Also the quilts let them know which houses were safe to go to for help. The quilts were often hung on porches or fences so that the runaways could see them easily.

Many times the only safe shelter was a cold, dark, cellar in a house. They had to stay there all day and be very quiet. They were very hungry and thirsty at times, but could only come up at night when they would not be discovered.

Friendly people helped the former slaves find food, water, clothing, shelter, and safe houses to stay in. They were the Abolitionist, the Masons, and many others. There were both white and free black people who made up these groups.

There were several boat captains, both white and black, who helped carry people to their new lives by boat or ship. It was quicker, easier, and safer to make the long journey by sea when possible.

THE UNDERGROUND RAILROAD ILLUSTRATIONS

1. COTTON PLANTATION
2. STEALING AWAY
3. WADE IN THE WATER
4. APPALACHIAN MOUNTAIN TRAIL
5. FOLLOW THE NORTH STAR
6. SPRINGTIME FOREST
7. NORTH STAR QUILT
8. DOWN IN THE CELLAR
9. ABOLITIONIST GUIDE
10. BY LAND AND SEA

ILLUSTRATIONS PAINTED BY LOUISE CHESSI MCKINNEY
2005
ACRYLIC ON CANVAS (16 X 20 IN.)

Underground Railroad Quilt Squares Coloring Book

Quilts often acted as signs that instructed the escaping slaves on how to run to freedom without being caught. They told them how to get ready for the long journey, what to do, and where to go. The quilts were placed near slave cabins on the plantation, thrown over fences, porches, balconies, and displayed in churches. Each quilt told the slaves to take a certain action when it was on view. This secret form of communication allowed the slaves to alert each other as to when, who, and by what means they were escaping. Only one quilt would be displayed at a time, so that no one but the slaves would know what was really taking place. The whole code would be memorized by using a sampler quilt with patterns arranged in order of the code.

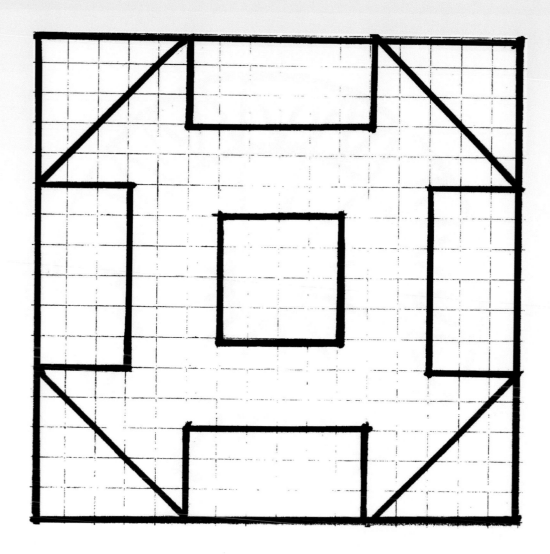

Monkey Wrench

The monkey wrench quilt pattern told the slaves to gather all of the tools they would need on their journey. This pattern also refers to a leader who would get things started such as a blacksmith, a sailor, an abolitionist, or a black preacher. It may also represent the famous writer and orator Frederick Douglass, who had access to a network of people from the South to the North. A monkey wrench quilt is displayed on a bed in <u>The Frederick Douglass House</u> in Washington D.C.

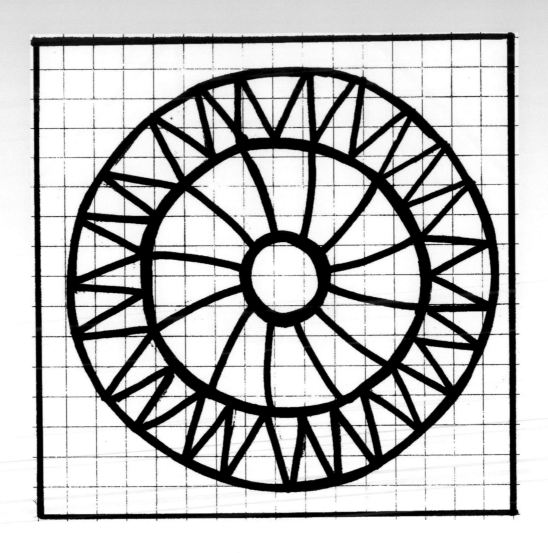

Wagon Wheel

The Wagon wheel pattern signaled the slaves to pack all of the things that would go into the wagon, or that would be used in moving. This pattern also has religious significance in that Jesus was a carpenter, and many spirituals and songs told the slaves to "steal away" or "run away" to Jesus and therefore to go northwest. The sun was also viewed as a blazing wheel of fire descending behind the Appalachian Mountains in the west, toward Ohio.

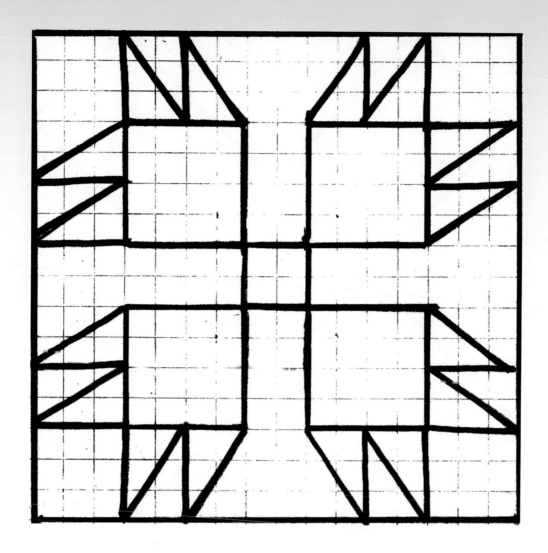

Bear's Paw

The bear's paw pattern helped the runaway's to know to follow the tracks left by bears to navigate their way through the mountains. This was similar to a road map. Most escapes took place in the Spring when bears were roaming the forest along rivers and streams which provided a supply of water and fish. The code says that <u>wagon wheel</u> traveled on a bear's paw trail to the <u>crossroads.</u>

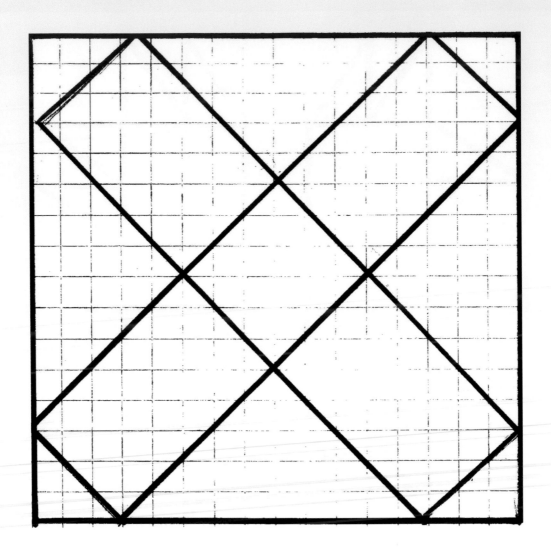

Crossroads

The crossroads pattern consists of basic shapes arranged in a way that is similar to the mapping of plantation. The crossroads has been identified as Cleveland, Ohio; and the region of Ohio called the Firelands was known to have a large bear population. The wagon wheels followed the bear's paw trail through the mountains to the crossroads to Cleveland. The crossroads also represents the making of life changing choices and decisions, which the slaves made on their escape to freedom.

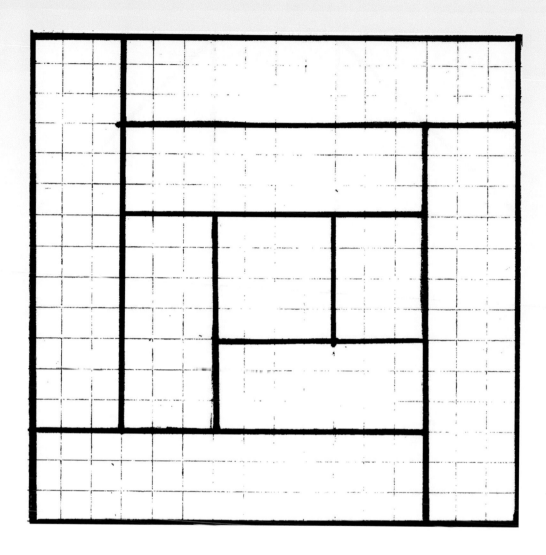

Log Cabin

The log cabin pattern is shown with a light colored center to represent the function of the cabin as a light or beacon in the wilderness such as a safe house. Also the pattern shows the connection between the white and black Masons since it helped the slaves to know with whom it was safe to communicate. Some of these persons were <u>Prince Hall Masons</u> who were familiar with African and American symbols. Slaves were often aided by free black Masons who had their own society.

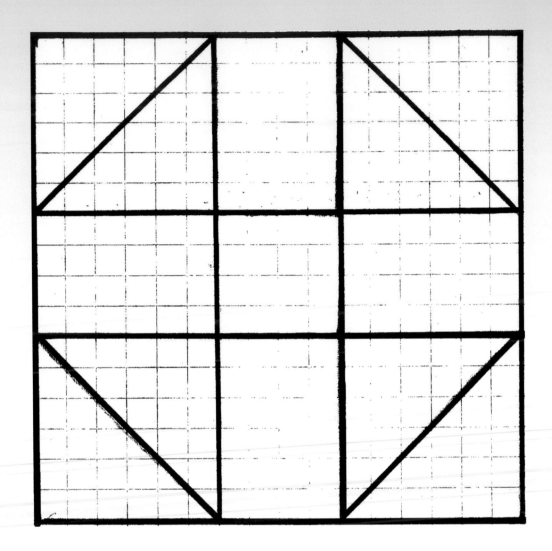

Shoofly

The shoofly pattern referred to a person who helped the escaping slaves. This was most likely a free black person or a Mason who was familiar with a secret language. Since the language and structure of Masonic orders are geometrically based, it was the perfect way to create and hide the code in plain wiew and make it easy for "shoofly" to direct the action at his point.

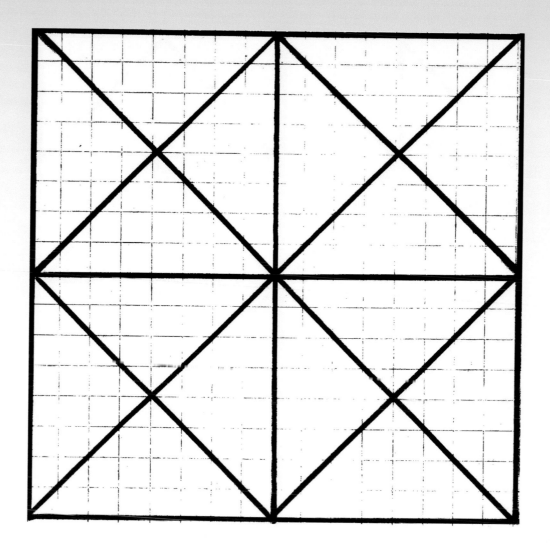

Bow Tie

Through the bow tie pattern the slaves were told to "get dressed up in cotton and satin bow ties and go to church and exchange double wedding rings". This meant to dress in formal clothes which was usually given to them by other free blacks. Once the clothes were exchanged, the slaves could go places with the free black citizens undetected. They could go to the church and get help removing their chains, as represented by the double wedding rings.

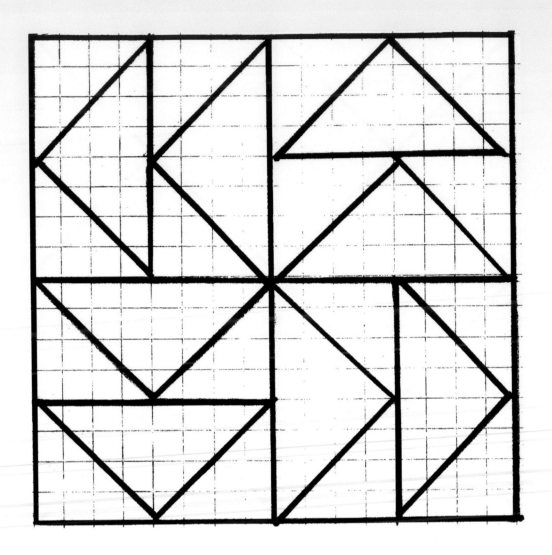

Flying Geese

The flying geese pattern gave the slaves clues about direction, timing, and behavior based on the migrating geese. Geese fly north in the spring or summer so the people knew what direction to travel, and the best season to leave in. Since geese stop at rivers and streams to rest and eat, this design told the slaves to do the same.

Zig-Zag path

The zig-zag path pattern was a clear warning for slaves to move in a crooked line when traveling and to double check occasionally in their tracks. This was done in order to confuse any slave hunters who might be following them. A zig-zag line from Charleston, South Carolina would have brought the slaves to Dresden, Ohio which is in Coshocton County. The zig-zag path could have very well run from the plantations near Charleston up through Coshocton County.

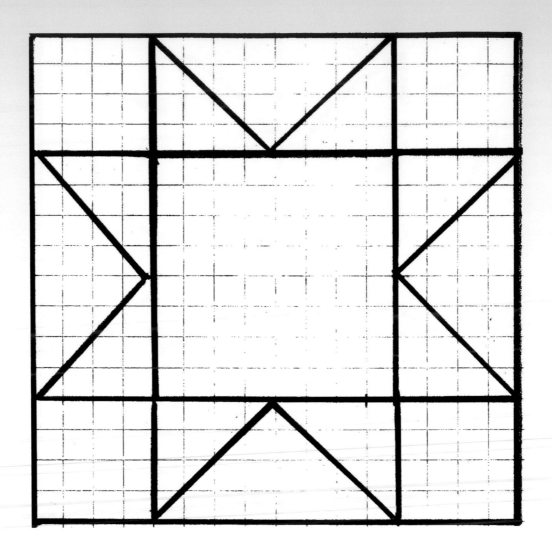

North Star

The north star was probably the most used, and also the most recognized quilt in the Underground Railroad code. The north star has always been critical to navigation on the seas as well as land. It was the subject of the folk song called Follow the Drinking Gourd in which orders are given to follow the points of the "drinking gourd – the Big Dipper – to the brightest star, the North Star. The 'drinking gourd" or Big Dipper always points to the North Star, which is located in the handle of the Little Dipper. This eight – pointed star is one that folklore and oral history honor as a guiding light for traveling slaves. To them it must have seemed like the star of Bethlehem.

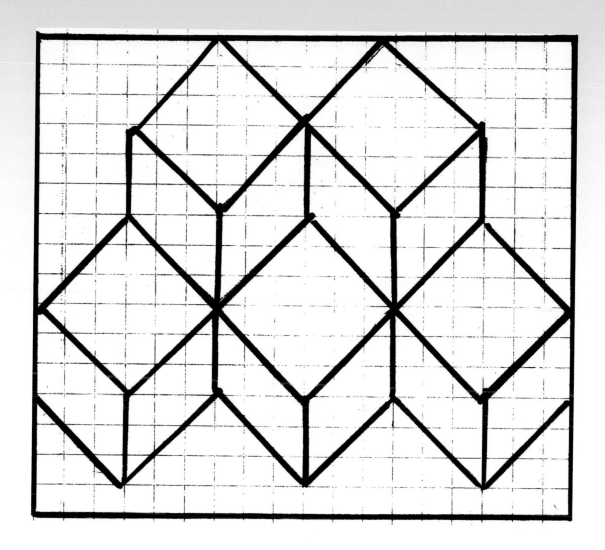

Tumbling Blocks

The tumbling blocks pattern was one of the quilts used in the end of the journey because of the association of boxes with packing and moving. When this quilt was displayed it was the signal for the slaves to pack their belongings, and to avoid possible trouble the closer they got to the north.

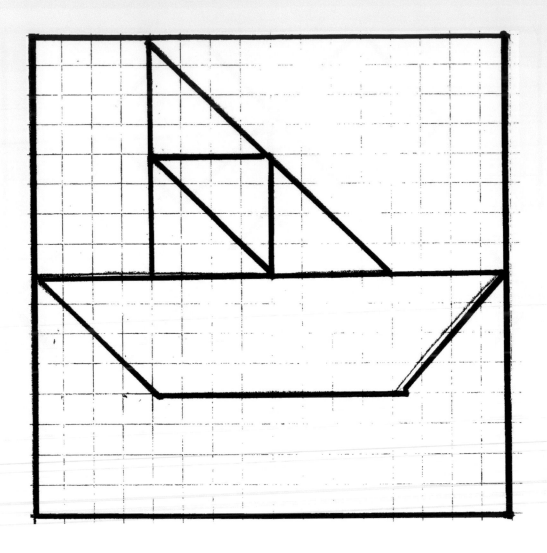

Sail Boat

The sailboat pattern represented routes slaves took by sea, lake, river, and canal. Specialized boat service existed between Chicago and Detroit. Several boats ran between Sandusky, Ohio and Detroit. They were the Arrow, the United States, and the Walk-in-the-Water. Other boats serving Cleveland and Detroit included the Forest Queen and the Morning Star. Many slaves received help from free black sea captains and sailors such as William Wells Brown who was a steamboat captain on Lake Erie for nine years.

GLOSSARY

Abolitionist - a person who wants to put an end to slavery.

Appalachian Mountains - a mountain range extending from eastern Canada to central Alabama.

Big Dipper - a cluster of seven stars forming the shape of a cup with a long handle.

Blacksmith - a person who forges and shapes iron with an anvil and hammer.

Crossroads- a place where two or more roads meet.

Drinking Gourd - the dried and hollowed-out shell of a pumpkin or squash used as a cup for drinking.

Frederick Douglass - African-American abolitionist, writer, and orator. He was born a slave in 1817, but escaped to the North at the age of 21.

Geometrically - application of surface shapes in a measured configuration involving the relationships of points, lines, and angles.

Little Dipper - a smaller version of the Big Dipper.

North Star - a star at the end of the handle of the Little Dipper.

Overseer - a person who watched over the plantation and directed the work of the slaves.

Plantation - a large estate or farm on which crops such as cotton, were raised and harvested by African slaves.

Prince Hall Masons - members of the first black Masonic Lo©e, made up of free blacks in the time of slavery and known today as black Masons.

Quilt - a blanket made by stitching two layers of cloth together with padding In between.

Sampler guilt - a quilt made up of all of the patterns which tell the Underground Railroad route.

Slave - a human being who is forced into servitude as the property of a person or household.

Spiritual - a religious song of African- American origin.

Zigzag - a course of movement consisting of sharp turns in alternating directions.

SOURCES

The American Heritage Dictionary- Third Edition. NewYork: Dell Publishing, 1994.

Franklin, John Hope. An Illustrated History of Black Americans. New York:
Time-Life Books, 1970.

Tobin, Jacqueline L., and Raymond G. Dobard, Ph.D. Hidden in Plain View: A Secret Story of Quilts and the Underground Railroad (as told by Ozella McDaniel Williams). New York: Anchor Books- a division of Random House, inc., 2000.

Printed in the United States
By Bookmasters